LIVING ON
PURPOSE

LIVING ON
PURPOSE

10 KEYS TO DISCOVERING
YOUR PURPOSE AND
EXPANDING YOUR POTENTIAL

VINCENT ROBINSON

LIVING ON **PURPOSE**

Vincent Robinson Ministries
rightayccc.org
ISBN 978-0-9890267-3-4

Published by RMP Group

Acknowledgements

I am so appreciative of what God is doing in my life and in the ministry of Right Way. I want to thank the love and joy of my life, my wife – Mishondia. You are my best friend, life and ministry partner, and none of this births forth without you. To the best kids a man could ask for: Darius, Kierstin, Kirah and Kennedy and my grandson Jayden. You guys mean the world to me and I hope that my life sets an example worth following. To my Right Way family: You guys are the greatest! The love and support you show MiShondia and me is unparalleled. We love you and are totally committed to our assignment of leading and teaching you in the things of God. To Cheryl Martin. I'm telling ya - everybody needs a friend like you. I am thankful for you being in my life and ministry. And to Julie King. Your new name is lifeboat.

To purposed people! To greatness in you. And to whom all blessing flow - the Source, Energy and person with whom I live for to see and hear say, "Well done, thou good and faithful Servant" - Jesus Christ.

dear reader,

To me, writing a book is a huge undertaking. In my line of work, we not only give encouragement and answers to life issues but we are also held accountable for helping people reach their full potential and to me that is a humbling assignment. One of my greatest passions is people. I love to see people discover who they were created to be and help them tap into those skills and special qualities that no school or university can give. I believe that God did His finest work when He made man, and we should be the reflection of that great work. We are all created and gifted with greatness, and it's that discovery that makes life fulfilling. It is from the Creator Himself that we find out our purpose, and sometimes it just takes the right words, moment or book to help unlock what has been lying dormant for so long.

That is what I want this book to do. I want it to give life and hope to what you desire to do the most. I want it to set or relight a fire in the hearts of those who have failed and help them realize that it's worth the cost to try and if need be, try again. And lastly, I want this book to help you find the path that you so desire - Success. We are all unique. And I believe that it is that uniqueness that we work out of that gives what we do meaning and the creativity that sets it apart from others and even those that are doing the same. There is room and a place for everyone - let's discover yours.

Consider this book as my personal letter to you. As I looked back over my life, I began to recognize that the signal of success was always being transmitted to me. I am now doing things that I ignored as a young man and even passed by. And had I had true success in mind, that was an out birth of my purpose rather than temporary fame, a guide who had been there or even knowledge of what to look for, I would have given those moments more attention. And even though they were small, the return would have far outweighed the initial investment.

I want to be that guide to show you how to see the signs, help put success in right perspective for you, and help you recognize when the signal of success is being transmitted to you. Both failure and success are optional, and you decide which one you'll have. I know once you discover your purpose; there will be an optimism to see it develop, while at the same time an apprehension of doing what's needed. It is my prayer that you will begin to value your time, talent and treasure and use these to your benefit and betterment. If you can see it, you can become it. Let me repeat that. If you can see it, you can become it! And my only charge to you is that you don't let it stop with you. Pour into someone else for their personal success, wanting nothing in return but that they carry on with the same charge. You are now on the right track. From this moment forward, I want you to see success not as something that you have to become, but success as who you are. You are in your birthing season, and its name will be Greatness.

table of contents

introduction

IT'S IN THERE! You've been equipped with a distinct DNA. And although everyone on earth has blood, your blood sets you apart from billions of others. It identifies only you. Purpose is the same way. Everybody has one, but what you have is given to identify only you. The other great thing is we don't have to look far to find it because it starts right inside of us. Society teaches us to find the hottest thing going and ride it out. This type of *success deception* holds no long term promise, and it takes from your dreams the dedication and work it would take for them to come into being. It's no different than a robbery, except it's you you're robbing.

The Creator has already put success in you. You were created for it. No one can say they don't have it. Having success, versus cultivating and developing that success is the difference maker. Within all of us, God placed purpose. He then gave each of us talents, skills and giftings that give life to that purpose. For what you are called to do you are already qualified.

The goal of *Living On Purpose* is to get you to see that you have a purpose and that in every day, there is success for that purpose. Everything you do, down to resting and exercise is all a part of you arriving to that place of purpose. To get you to see that with every day and with every decision, you are either stagnant, moving towards or moving away from living in your purpose. It is with our everyday successes that bring us into purpose. That means that you are in a Season of Success all the time although it may not seem like it. Some seasons may have you in a position of rest and reset while what you've already done has taken root for what you have to do next, but you are always in a season! So even NOW there is something you should be doing. Waiting isn't sitting around. The waiter or waitress - waits on you. That means they are serving you based on the order given. Well, your purpose is always speaking, alerting and pointing you in the right direction. This could be a certain desire to do something or simply following a plan of action.

The reality is - you were not created to fail. Think about it: the only things that hurt are those things that aren't supposed to happen. That's why I can say that you weren't created to fail because failure hurts.

Start Here
like NOW

So what are you waiting on? Are you waiting for the doorbell to ring and everything you ever desired to be is standing there? Or maybe one morning you'll just wake up and find yourself dropped right smack dab in the middle of your purpose? Do you have the "It's Gonna Happen" syndrome? I would hope that none of these are your thoughts about being successful and walking in your purpose because if so, pinch yourself because you are definitely asleep or daydreaming.

The truth of the matter is that purpose happens on purpose. I would like to further submit to you that right now you are *in purpose*. Yea, right now! You may not be doing exactly what your purpose requires or even have knowledge on what your purpose is, but at this very moment you are in purpose because you are that purpose. Remember, everyone has purpose. Most people see purpose and success as something that they have to attain rather than seeing purpose and success as something that they are. However, not being aware of it doesn't mean you don't have it.

I can say you have it now because nothing that has to do with you walking in purpose or being a success will come from outside of you. Take a moment and think about what I just said because most people spend all their lives looking outside of themselves when the one single thing they need to first discover is within them. It's possible for others to see it but no one can tell you what your purpose is. And no matter how it comes, this is *the one thing* in your life that *you have to discover.* Whether it's through reading of books, information from conferences, the overview of advice or whatever vehicle you use. With all that taken together, it will still come from within.

> the greatest fulfillment in life is being in purpose

Also, don't be mistaken in believing that only the educated have purpose. There are many who are educated far beyond the scope of average, yet they aren't walking in their purpose, so we can't attribute it to simply being the most educated. It is those who have identified their purpose, set eyes on their dreams, and who capitalize on every opportunity presented that are the ones who see success. Because they understand that they are NOW somewhere in the stream of their purpose, they make the best of even a rainy day. Just because there are no leaves on the tree doesn't mean that it's not alive. It's just in a different season, which calls for the shedding of leaves and not the growth of them. The tree is as alive NOW as it would be in the summer when full of leaves.

Right NOW you are in purpose. I don't care if you don't have a dime or dollar to your name and your life looks like it is at its lowest. Because you haven't discovered your purpose doesn't mean that you aren't in it. Maybe you know your purpose and have yet to do anything to create the momentum that it needs to take off. But neither of these determine whether or not you are in purpose. The moment you grasp that you are a purpose being, the game changes. You no longer look for something to do - you discover who you are; the beginning of purpose.

Take a moment right now and do this exercise. Take a sheet of paper and write down all the things you like to do. Now cross out anything that you couldn't see yourself doing for a long period of time. Next, cross out those things that don't help others. Now, put two lines under everything that makes you smile and includes helping someone else in some way. Lastly, circle those things that come natural to you. Although you may have to have schooling, these things make you feel alive. Now those things underlined are streams (you'll learn about that later). The ones circled have to do with your purpose. Now pray about it and see which ones agree with your inner man. All that's left is for you to determine what NOW can I be doing?

defining the river

The bird has flying in him. The fish has swimming in him. And like the bird and the fish, there is a creative uniqueness in you. There is something that you are ordained to master. It's called your river. It's your purpose. Defining the river is about discovering your unique purpose in life. But why a river? One reason I call it a river is because a river gives and supplies life to inner areas, and purpose does the same. Secondly, I call it the river because people often find streams in life before they find their river. A stream is that temporary thing that you do that leads you into your river (purpose). The stream is not who you are but what you do until you come into the fullness of who you are. The difference is that rivers feed streams - streams don't feed rivers. For that reason it is important that you define your river.

It is possible that you may be currently in a stream which is not a bad thing at all. However, it can become dangerous when you acquire too much while at the stream stage. I call this "Banking on the Stream". This can be one of life's biggest casualties because when the time comes that you define your river and need to transition, you can't because you have too many things that you've attached to the supply of the stream, and can't let it go in order to transition into your river. Many people are in this state and so desperately desire to go after their purpose, but they have so many things dependent upon what's already coming. Consequently, they are too afraid to make needed steps or worse yet, can't move at all. So they feel trapped and robbed of life.

It is a feeling of enslavement to see your river but be unable to apprehend it because you are trapped in the stream. I am not one of the ones who believes in having to lose it all in order to become the authentic you. If those who share this situation of possibly losing it all would be honest, they, in error, banked on the stream. You shouldn't live in the stream like you should in the river. Now knowing this, what you should do is live within your means of knowing that right now you're only in a stream, and when you find out what your river is, then you don't have to lose it all for success. It is at this point, you can make the transition with ease. River defining is important because it is from the river that we receive current or might I say currency. This is why I say don't hang your success on a stream while you are defining your river.

The River

So you are now asking "what is my river?" As I stated earlier, the river is your purpose in life. I define purpose as a river because it's the source that delivers and the supply that restores, the flow that generates and the life that contributes. A stream needs the current of a river to improve the quality of its existence. But a river has within it the ability to be the stream, the river and much more; the ability to be a fulfilled purpose.

The discovery of one's purpose is one of the single most important discoveries in life. When purpose is unknown, the misuse of a thing and the diminishing of it are inevitable. Mistakes in life are inescapable but outside its purpose, mistakes are like throwing darts with a hope that the target is out there. When purpose is known, you have a target that you can not only see but also shoot for with the confidence and assurance of hitting. Very few people I meet in my line of work appear to be flowing in their river. Most are in unreasonable surmounting debt, depressed or not enjoying life. Instead, I meet people every day, in my line of work who are in streams. They have yet to define their river: their purpose. I believe this occurs because: 1 - Purpose demands that you hold yourself to a higher standard of order. 2 - Purpose pulls the best out of you. 3 - You receive in purpose, by way of its current: what you work for to get in streams.

Streams feel like work and that's because it is. This doesn't mean you may not enjoy them, but they require work. The river or your purpose isn't work. How much work do you think the fish puts into swimming or the bird into flying? It is work in the sense of the movement required but it's the motion of work - what it naturally does - versus the exerting of work to survive. See your river is what you can do with ease. No river struggles to move. There is a current constantly moving through it that carries it wherever it needs to go and your purpose in life is designed to do the same for you.

The one way you define your river is to ask yourself "What is it that I love to do? What would I do, if money wasn't an issue?" You see, the foundation of purpose is love. You should do what you do because you have a passion and love for it and not for the money or wealth that it may bring. When you are truly operating in purpose, money is automatic.

Next I want to challenge you to look back over your life. I've learned that in the early stages of life, purpose always finds its way of rearing its head. See, purpose can be an innate ability and creativity to do a thing without any prior training or help. As a child, my mom use to wake me up out of my sleep and make me preach and sing on a footstool.

> when what you do helps others and brings total fulfillment to you, you have discovered purpose.

That was my purpose crying out. Although they saw it as a joke, it was so natural to me that I could wake up from my sleep and do it. Whenever we played house as kids, I was always the one who wanted to stand and speak to the people. Unbeknown to me at the time, that was my river.

Fast-forward, I now pastor one the most progressive churches in the South. I host an international TV program and write books and study manuals through my own book company. I founded and teach an in-house Bible Institute while traveling and speaking to thousands and counseling many. All that was in me but it took me discovering my river so that the many streams could flow from me. Notice I said streams. There are other streams that can be in your life that are different from the ones mentioned earlier. Now that you are in your river, you can have multiple streams operating out of your river. Remember, earlier when we spoke of streams, there was no river. But once you start operating in your river, you can have branches of streams bringing additional revenues back into your river. Remember that the river comes first. This means that the river has precedence over everything. The one thing that doesn't change is that you don't bank on the stream.

So, in defining your river, think of what you would do if money wasn't an issue. Evaluate your life to see what thing you played with the most. Ask yourself the big question "What do I like to do to help others?" What most people don't realize is that purpose is mostly about you helping and not getting. The reason most never find their purpose is because they are only looking for those things from which they can benefit from. But the moment you examine how you like to help others - something comes alive.

Lastly, whether you believe it or not you should pray. I believe that we are divinely created and what better person to ask than the Creator Himself. The key is being patient and humble enough to hear.

Be the Entrepreneur

It is my goal that this book will inspire you. But more importantly, I want this challenge to connect with the entrepreneur in you. I also want it to confront those inner barriers that you allow to keep you from being the best you, you can be. If you can think it, you can do it. I believe that there is a spirit of entrepreneurship in every single person walking the earth. The problem is that many people are afraid to "pop the top", or they lack the ambition to go for it. They like the play it safe approach. But no one who is successful just plays it safe.

Dell founder Michael Dell got his start working as a dishwasher in a Chinese restaurant and started PCs Limited in his dorm room. He dropped out of college at 19 and is now worth billions. People look at Walmart now and are in awe, but no one remembers the time when Sam Walton was poor and milking cows and doing daily paper runs. He opened his first general store with only $20,000 dollars, only $5,000 being his own. Today, the Walton Family and the Walmart Stores are worth billions. Daymond John, the CEO of FUBU, saw a grand opportunity and took full advantage of it. While working fulltime at Red Lobsters restaurant, he started at home sewing his logo on hats, T-shirts and jerseys and selling them for profit. Through dedication and hard work, FUBU grew to be a number one company in urban apparel. And lastly there is a gentleman who always dreamed of being a speaker and author. He wrote his first book and sent it to a major book company and they turned him down. He'd see other people receiving speaking engagements but nothing seemed to gain traction for him. The one time he had an opportunity to speak the guy before him went over his time and they almost canceled him. Because he was nice and understood, the people gave him five minutes to address a packed house of students. Those five minutes that became three, turned into speaking engagements not only around town but calls started to come in from other states. He now travels quite often and speaks to thousands.

> leaders lead, no matter where they are or what they are doing.

Moreover, the rejector of the book company pushed him to learn how to publish a book himself. Now he has a book publishing company, has published seven books and helps others publish books. That person is me. I realized that if it were going to happen, I had to make it happen. Everybody doesn't get the handout, but everybody has a chance and I decided to capitalize on mine. I could not sit back and wait for others to approve what I knew I had the ability to do. I refused to sit my dream in the lap of someone and hope that they saw what I saw and would do it. Will you?

You live in the land of opportunity. There are many other success stories of those who started out at the bottom and made their way to the top. See, an entrepreneur is simply a person who organizes and manages any enterprise, especially a business with considerable initiative and risk. So long before the company or business becomes something that all will see, you are that entrepreneur when it's right in the corner of your bedroom, on your laptop, or while you are working for someone else. Leaders lead no matter where they are or what they are doing. Put them anywhere and they possess this unique skill to rally the crowd towards the common goal, or if left alone can complete the task without overhead observance.

That's what you have. Certain people pick up certain books. And if this book caught your eye it's because I am talking to people like you. You have what it takes - you just have to ignore the size right now and take what you have and work it. Don't focus on its current size; focus on the potential of the size it can become.

I speak to the greatness inside of you. And I command it to come alive. Every dormant dream has to live. I strip away the power of every failed attempt or timidity to even try. You Will do great things! You Will have success! You Will walk in your purpose! YOU WILL WIN!

the belief in self

Success and failure start in the same place - inside. Successful people have to believe that they are before they become. On your journey to becoming your created self, you will face many pitfalls and roadblocks and even some failures. But it's that inner witness of believing that you are destined for success that will give you the fortitude to turn obstacles, stumbling blocks and even failures into stepping stones to your divine appointed destiny. Earlier, if you recall, I said that I am a pastor. Now, in the church community there is this statement that many believe "if you have Jesus, you have all you need". But I submit to you, that there are people who have Jesus and are sincere in their devotion to Him but aren't successful. And then there are those who don't have Jesus and are very successful. See, having or not having Jesus doesn't mean anything if you don't believe that you are [right now] a successful person.

Many believe that you have reached the ladder of success when you have something to show for it. But this is so far from the truth. Success starts when you have nothing but a determination, a will and an unwavering belief in self that you can accomplish whatever you set your mind to. The stuff is just the outcome of what you believed all the time. If it is not for believing that you can, you will never see the potential of what believing can produce.

No one can make you believe in you. Believing in self is not arrogance, pride or selfishness. It is a much needed component in obtaining success. Like I said earlier - success and failure start in the same place, so you either believe you can and you will or you don't and you won't. You will be amazed at the number of people who have a clear awareness on what they should be doing but have an overwhelming fear of doing it. They have a fear of success. They are no different than a person who is afraid of heights. Do you know that most people who are afraid of heights have never been up high enough to even look down? So as strange

> it's hard to receive the encouragement from others, if you don't first believe in self.

as it may seem, they fear up and have never been there. It's just looking that way that grips them. And this is the same fear that overcomes a person when they don't believe in themselves.

Belief is the springboard of your dreams, aspirations and success. Ask any successful person what his/her greatest obstacle was and most will tell you that it was believing that he or she could. But you may be saying "Well, I do believe in me". But do you? Seeing what you want and seeing you having it is not believing. There will be times where your purpose will require your last dime. Times when purpose will require you to do something that you've never done and possibly have had no training to do - will you do it? Pause and think long before you answer. See, many people say they believe in themselves but when it comes to making those transitioning decisions, one gets to see where their belief lies.

Everybody lines up at the starting line but everybody doesn't run the race. Will the size of the mountain defeat you because you've never before had to climb as high? There was a show on TV called *Fear Factor*. The objective of the show was to push the person's belief by making them face their fears. Now, going in, every person believed that they could win, but it was when the challenge showed up that the belief was truly tested. The contestants had several levels to go through and at each level the contestant with the worst performance fell off until you finally had a winner. There were some who quit before they even competed because fear became the factor. What am I saying? Success is like the Fear Factor television show - everybody wants to play but when faced with the challenge, fear rather than believing becomes the factor.

No one is going to just hand success over to you. Dreams don't just come to pass. There is work involved. I want you to remember this next statement:

What you see is always the result of what's in you.

What does this statement mean? It means you can only produce to the degree of how much you believe you can. The whole of your life is the sum total of how much you believe in you. Even God the Father who has no limits is limited by how much you believe. He says *if you can believe all things are possible to him that believeth.* So the ability to do strongly rests in believing you can.

Before you start the quest of pursuing success, get your belief in you in check. You are your most valuable player. The play [vision/dream] was given to you. It's one thing to believe in the play, but it's a whole different thing to believe that you can complete it. Don't just believe it - Believe in you.

Know Your Worth

Another thing that plays into your belief in self is knowing your worth. Unlike products that are at the grocery store that come prepackaged and already priced with a shelf life, the only person who defines your worth is you. What are you worth?

I used to own a barbershop and after several years of getting paid the same thing, I decided that the service I was rendering was worth more than what I was getting. I was worth more. I wanted to go up in price but felt it would be easier if all the barbershops did it together. So on a not so busy day, I went around to all the major shops and told the barbers what I was planning on doing to see if they were willing to buy in also. Well, needless to say, as much as they wanted to, they were afraid that they would lose customers to other barbers in town who would stay at the original price. Although agreeing that they deserved more, they allowed the common feeling of complacency to have rule over their knowing of worth. Thus they were actually allowing others to gauge their worth.

> I want to pause here in the story to interject a point and that is when you know your worth you have to be willing to run when others want to walk.

Having no success with the other shops, I decided to step out on my own. I planned it by letting my customers know in advance the price change and on what date this would take place. It would be a whopping $4 dollar increase per cut. Guess what, the majority of my customers got on board. I had several customers who were happy for me. They even said "I was wondering why you were so cheap." And yes, I did lose some customers. That's the price you pay for knowing your worth. If you are ever fearful of lost, you won't qualify for gain. The price change compensated for those who left. But months later, those same customers who left, after realizing that it was worth it or let me say I was worth what I was asking, came back and became more loyal and committed. After the news got out around town that I had gone up and business was yet booming, the rest of the city caught on and went up too.

What's your worth? What if I had capitulated from what I knew to be the right thing for me; not because others were doing it but because I deserved it? I couldn't take my success and gauge it against what others wanted but were not bold enough to do because they could yet see it in themselves. Regardless of what anyone else thinks, regardless of what others have said about you or even how they see you, what do you see? WHAT'S YOUR WORTH?

Why do you buy name brand items? There are knockoff brands in everything imaginable. Why do you pay extra money? And why don't the name brands come down to compete with the price of the no-name brands? See, you will either see yourself as a name that you will brand and others will buy, or you will be a knockoff. You have to know your worth. This is important because it will set the barometer for your circle of influence. People hang with those with whom they believe appropriate the pinnacle of where they want to go. Eagles never fly with buzzards - not even for fun. And buzzards never try to fly as high as eagles.

Raise the Success Ceiling

You may not know it but there is an invisible ceiling over your head. We all have one. And you set the summit of this ceiling by the conviction of your own personal worth. Knowing this is important because this ceiling will gauge your work habits and even the audaciousness at which you go after things. Many people don't reach high because their success ceiling isn't high. Don't operate under a low ceiling of success - raise it! Donald Trump doesn't just buy land - he buys air. When he purchases land for a building, he sets the bar of how high other buildings can build around him so as to not block the beautiful views that he wants to offer to his clients. Other developers didn't think like that. That's why he's a top developer. Don't become a victim of allowing your surroundings to set the height of your success ceiling. You always keep high expectations.

This is valuable information when it comes to the people you hang around. I live in what should be one of the number one port cities in the United States. But ironically, we always get things last. Two of the main federal interstates travel through my city, but we offer very few attractions to catch the attention of those travelers. Many people grow up here and leave to start businesses elsewhere, and some become very successful. But I don't allow the climate of the city's ceiling to have an effect on how high I can set my ceiling. Nor do I measure my success by those who are doing what I do. Maybe that's as high as they want to go, or maybe they have become contaminated by the city's ceiling. Either way, how high I want to go is up to me. It's never the size of the city but the ceiling in the person.

What's your ceiling? The cliché "the sky is the limit" is true, but where is your ceiling in the sky? You'll never know what it is until you know your worth.

Self-Investment

When a person believes in him/herself, it's not only a thought but it's proven. That person is the initial investment. You should be your first investor. Never look for a hand-up if you aren't reaching upward. Don't assume that just because you've shared your dream that others are going to automatically pitch in. Purposed people are automatically attracted to something that's moving. So if you aren't helping yourself, why should anyone else?

- **Keep learning** - I didn't say you have to know it all, but you should know something about it. You should know the numbers (if there are any), current mechanics, etc., for the field that you are aspiring to be a part of. What one book do you have that deals with the success you desire? Industries and the way of doing things constantly changes. And new things are added all the time. You want to make sure that you stay abreast and updated.

- **Stay Ahead** - What conference, summit, symposium can you attend that will keep you abreast. I am a huge proponent of conferences and seminars in the field of your expertise. They always stay ahead of the curve of any changes or new material that is soon to come. What company is at the top in that field? Who is the person leading the pack?

- **Give the Best** - Forming a habit is not hard. Breaking it presents the problem! You want to start with the habit of giving your best because how you start is usually how you continue. I have a motto that I stand by and it is:

> **I will do the best, use the best and give the best at whatever level I'm on.**

Just because you haven't reached the plateau of where you desire to be doesn't mean you just operate at a "just getting by" standard. You have to acquire an attitude of excellence which is a mindset that motivates one to choose to be and do his/her best, while giving attention to detail which results in above average living without compromising God given standards. You aren't just ordinary – you are extraordinary. You don't just give the 100%, you give 110%. With every effort, you strive for the maximum result.

You have a name that you are upholding and an integrity that you have to protect. **The reason why there aren't many at the top is not because there is not enough room, but because there are not many that are willing to do what's needed to get**

there and who stay there. At every level - Be your best - Do your best - Give your best. Be known for the best! That's how I live. This way of doing associates you with greatness long before you get there because greatness is more than a place, it's a way of being and doing things.

- **Be on time** - Time is one of the greatest commodities given to man. You should not be a waster of your time or anyone else's. A lack of being on time is the result of not having discipline. There is a reason why some people succeed and some people don't. Some people have missed their greatest moments because they didn't respect time. If there is one thing you want to respect, make sure it's time. Being on time demonstrates that you are prepared. Renew your mind to the importance of being on time. Be observant on what matters you make important. And most importantly, declutter your life. Late people have a tendency to make non-important matters important. When you are always late many things happen: personal goals, visions and purposes go unfulfilled, promotions are nullified, favor is denied, increase is expunged, you can't be trusted, you destroy the morale of others, you cultivate the wrong attitude, you destroy the integrity of the company or business and make managerial staff look bad, profits diminish, things cost more, you quit life because of false perceptions, you become a candidate for trouble, you will cut corners on important procedures and you give partial productivity. Time is important. Make it important to you.

- **Keep your word** - I don't care how much money you have, if your word can't be trusted your money means nothing. My grandfather was the first person I told that I heard the call to preach. I just knew that he was going to give me this long speech of what and what not to do. He was my hero. Well, my granddad had only one statement and it's the single most important advice I've ever received. I hold it very dear to my heart. He said "Don't be a lying preacher son. Your word is all you have."

If you say you are going to do something, do it! If you give your word on something there will be times that you will still have to do it even if it is an inconvenience to you, for no other reason than you gave your word. Your word speaks of your character and integrity. While many people can ruin your reputation only you can destroy your integrity. And when you are known for not keeping your word – in simpler terms - you are a man or woman who lacks character.

- **Look your best** - Don't be fooled, appearance does matter. And how you dress plays a key role in how you are received by others. What we are speaks of our character. What we do speaks of our performance. But how we look provides a snapshot of who we are. I had a gentleman I mentored in banking, and upon getting him to change his dress, he drew the attention of the manger which positioned him to not only get a raise but to also be promoted when he had not worked long enough for either. You are either going to drift with the convenient crowd or you are going to gallop with the leaders. I'm not saying go in debt buying clothes. That would be portraying an image that you aren't. But how you present yourself should mean something to you. You should step out representing you - the best you can. You are your personal billboard. There are people who are willing to hear you and give attention to what you have to offer for nothing else than your appearance alone. Become aware of what those in the environment you choose to travel in look for, not those who follow but those who lead. And even on your worst day, look your best. You never know who is watching.

These are those personal investments that you have to give yourself if you want to be successful. There may be more but if you would just begin to pay attention to these and perfect them, you will begin to see yourself at Success' door. You owe it to yourself to be the best you that you can be. Success doesn't come without a price and the first place of investment is in you.

Here are some things to avoid that can rob you of your belief in you.

1. Past failures - All of us have had and will have some failures. All failure is not failure. Real failure is to miss the mark and not try again. Don't allow a knockdown to become a knockout. Regroup - regain your focus and try again. At least you now know what not to do.

2. Size bullying - Listen, the same bones in the child are the same bones that are in the man - they've just grown. My point is nothing started out the size you now see it. The vision you have in mind is huge, but NEVER be moved by the size of a thing because you don't have to accomplish it all in a day. Most of our greatest wars weren't won by the size of the army but by the heart of the men who were fighting. Everything big shoulders the efforts of every small thing it took to get it there. See the size as your potential feat and not a downfall. No one ever saw themselves building a house in their dreams, although that's what they call it when they wake up. Dreams show the finish product so that when you come out of the dream you now know what all your efforts will accomplish and allow to keep before you what you are reaching for. The dream shouldn't frighten you because if you couldn't do it, you wouldn't have dreamt it.

Size bullying can also be self-inflicted when you look at the success of others and compare yourself to them. This is very dangerous and often leads to jealousy, fatalism and finding deceptive ways of skipping needed process for temporary fame. Stay focused on the lane you have to drive in and in time you'll arrive. Eighty percent of jealousy is admiration. Maybe if you drew closer, you could get some ideas that you could use to improve upon what you are already doing.

3. The "What if?" question - This is the most dangerous question that you can ask or try to answer. To answer you would have to go back and redo what you already have. It cancels all possibilities of trying again. The question holds the death certificate to what was once the potential to greatness. It is symbolic of a skydiver pulling his cord before he jumps or a scuba diver using his oxygen on the boat ride out to the dropping point - it robs you of all energies and resources to move. Its nicknames are fear and intimidation.

Never ask "what if" because it's a question that you cannot answer. Learn from any mistake. Pause only to collect salvageable data and quickly proceed to moving on.

4. Meeting the status quo - The only person you can be is you. If you are copying anyone you have already made yourself second. You are an original. I don't care how many people are doing it; no one can do it like you. Be the original. There is no pressure in being you - you are already good at it. I'm not saying that we don't look to others to improve on ourselves and receive wisdom and knowledge for our betterment. But we do not look to others to approve what the Creator Himself has uniquely given and empowered us to become. When you try to live up to the bar that others set, you fall short of the bar already set for you. You yield your power and creativity to the control of someone else saying "good job." Those who are out front have no more than you - they just decided not to run with the crowd.

i Believe

i Believe that there is greatness inside of me.

i Believe that I am equipped with all the necessary things to accomplish my purpose in life and handle any situation that comes my way.

i Believe that victory is always the outcome of what I set out to accomplish.

i Believe that in my path there are people who will help me reach my destiny and those who are against me will be made known so that in avoiding them, I am safe.

i Believe that when I help others - that same help is reciprocated back to me.

i Believe that as I meditate, I receive clear insight into the nature of a thing.

i Believe that I am always ahead and never behind.

i Believe that my attitude is one that is of humility and kindness and I never take anyone lightly; holding all men with the utmost respect even if I am mistreated.

i Believe that in each day, I have favor and good fortune.

i Believe that God is helping me become what He created me to be.

goal the vision

There is nothing that's more important to purpose than writing down your vision. But what's equally as important is that you goal that vision. The vision is the overall picture - the perceived outcome of a thing. The goals detail the steps that you are going to take to get there. In short, the vision is where you're going; the goal is how you're going to get there. It is foolish to assume that just because you see it, it will happen. I hope that you can hear this statement for how it was really meant to be interpreted *"everything happens for a reason"*. Oftentimes people use this statement to mean that it happened to prove a point or get you to see something; or even happened for your good. But that's not at all what that statement means. Simply put, what this statement has always meant is that everything happens because of something - a reason or cause. Reason speaks to an action. Everything is the outcome or reaction of the reason. It's saying that there was some action behind what happened, not some purpose.

There will be a reason why your vision comes to pass and the only reason it will come to pass is because you have purposefully planned for it to by setting goals. You've heard the statement "no one plans to fail - they just fail to plan". Well, this is a very true statement. I clearly remember putting one of my kid's Christmas gifts together for the first time. I tried to do it by only looking at the box (the vision). But to make sure that I would get what the box showed me, the manufacturer put a set of goals inside called instructions. Those instructions had a step by step process of showing me how I could arrive at what was on the box, safely. But I ignored them and thought that if I just looked at the box I could do it. There were objects that I had to snap on and once they snapped on, they were not supposed to come back off. There were also stickers that had this compound adhesive on them, so that once I put them on, they could stay on and uphold different weather conditions if left outside. But the instructions (goals) would tell me when the time was right to snap on and stick on. There was an order - a process that had to be respected if I wanted to see and experience what was on the box. But oh no, I just decided to go with looking at the vision. If I saw from the vision

> vision is the destination. goals are the streets and highways that get you there.

that an item was to go there, I'd put it there whether it was time to or not. See, goals stop the waste of energy and untimed steps. Goals set order around the vision so that you don't do something before time, having to only do it again at a later date. Needless to say, I totally messed up a perfectly good product. It wasn't that it was missing parts. It wasn't that I was presented one thing and got something else. It wasn't that something was wrong with the vision - the picture on the box. It was everything that it presented itself to be. I didn't follow the goals (instructions) that came with it.

Without proper planning, your vision will turn out just like my kid's toy, and you won't have anyone to blame but yourself. Many people have given up, are angry at life and feel unsuccessful and defeated for no other reason than they didn't take the time to plan out and set goals for what they wanted to see. They became so consumed with the vision, that finished product, that they didn't slow down long enough to address the putting together of the components. They try success by just looking at the box. Vison has to be goaled in order for it to come to pass!

Setting Goals

This is the bread-and-butter to success and vision fulfillment. If you get this part right, you are fast on your way. Do not start to do anything if you don't first have goals. There were times in my pursuit of purpose that I came across many roadblocks and sometimes those roadblocks became stopping points. At those times I felt like I wasn't achieving my goals. I found myself sitting around and I knew that I should have been doing something; I just never seemed to be able to figure out what that something was. At those moments I felt like success was escaping me and the little ground I had covered was escaping me as well. I would see the success of others that I admired and I would find myself becoming a bit jealous if not callous toward them and even a bit angry at God as if He was not moving fast enough in what I had done. Without goals, it's easy to find fault.

One day while sitting around, it hit me. I was sitting around. Before I had daily goals to accomplish, but now I didn't have anything to guide the efforts and energy of my day. I had this saying that if you don't give your day a direction your day will direct you which usually it leads to a dead end and that's exactly what I felt like. I realized what the problem was. Without goals I no longer had those short steps that led to the giant leaps that were causing the overall vision to come to pass. I felt failure because I no longer had the goals that perpetuated the temporary achievement that help to fortify me in my temporary state. Goals are temporary marks of success. They become the inner coach that says "you're winning – keep going"! Goals always show you what you should be doing NOW.

Seeing what needs to be done in order to see the vision come to pass can be chaotic. There is also this huge rush of zeal and sometimes haste to get it done. Zeal is good, but zeal with no guidance is deadly. A goal quiets the haste, takes zeal and sets the velocity so that you are able to hold on to the expectation of your desired outcome without rushing or doing something before its time, causing major setback that can compromise the vision. In setting goals they need to be:

1. Short and obtainable.

Know your limit. Don't bite off more than you can chew. Seeing a short list scratched off is better than a long list of incompletes. A shorter list completed keeps expectations high. A longer list, incomplete, makes the road look longer and oftentimes breeds procrastination.

Your goals also need to be obtainable. You have to be aware of where you are in purpose. This would also include your financial capabilities. I believe certain goals have a time attached to them, and when it's that time the needed resources will be at hand. If the goal isn't obtainable don't go into debt trying to make it come to pass. Do all you can do with what you have to do it with.

2. Practical

Certain goals need more attention than others, and you have to be honest with yourself with whether or not you are able to take on the challenge of what each goal demands. Be very practical in your approach. I believe in working hard but I also believe in working smart. I used to believe in storing up things - you may have called it getting ahead or moving something out of the way. And what I now realize is that when I finally got to the place where I could pull out the thing I got ahead on or stored up, I didn't need it or I didn't need it the way I did it. Allow each goal to have its proper time and place.

Perhaps some things can be done ahead of time. But if you learn patience and planning, things are just as good in their proper time.

3. Long term vs. short term

You will have long term goals and short term goals. A long term goal is a goal that needs accomplishing over a long period of time such as completing school, paying off a bill or losing a certain amount of weight. But short term goals are those things that you do day to day or week to week that play into the success of the long term goal. For example; setting aside twenty dollars a check to pay off the bill in 4 months or working out 3 times a week. Notice that without short term goals, you can't reach the long term goal.

I believe in using a very simple approach to this. Write down all the things you want or need to have done. Alongside them, write now or later. You've just simplified the list by clarifying which ones need to be done NOW. Next, take 2 to 4 of those items; knowing your limit, and develop goals to bring them to pass. Remember we need a short sheet because wins on short sheets look better than incompletes on long. Once you complete the list - celebrate by rewarding yourself and start over. Stick with the now side until the later side becomes the now.

Key Four

mandate the day

In everyday there are successes, failures, undertakings, adversity and opportunity. A major key to success is order. You have the capacity to determine how your day will turn out, and when you don't purposefully give your day a direction, you have automatically given the day the right to be whatever it wants. Your everyday should have a direction that it's going to go because you are going to give it one. Successful people don't sit back and see what the day is going to bring; for even the bird looks for the worm. They on purpose plan out their day, setting the tone and expectation of what each hour will consist of. Yes, you will have circumstances to occur that are out of your control, but the day itself shouldn't be out of control simply because you allowed it by not giving it a mandate. Successful people plan for success!

> the success of each day comes from the direction it's given.

If you don't know where you are going, how will you know when you get there? And if you ever expect to see success, you must plan your way there. Success doesn't just happen. Success is the outcome of a plan. A plan with purpose! A written plan

37

evokes a belief that mutes the wrong sensory perception. Not only does it mandate your day but it arouses a certain discipline and attitude of "get it done" in you. Planning pushes you to your toes and off your heels. No day should be without a plan. Even when you are going to rest, plan it.

When planning, don't go with a long to do list. A list of 5 to 7 things is good because this permits applicable time to accomplish each of them so that they are not rushed and you are doing it with excellence and not through haste. None of this is hard. If you are truly hungry for success, you will develop the discipline that other successful people had to. Mandate your day by giving it a direction. Time is a very important commodity, and if not careful, as the old saying goes, "It can escape you". So by mandating your day you set an order and direction for the day so that at the end you can call it a "Successful Day".

The D's of the Day

Success is a choice. And if this is the choice you've made then there are some behavioral things that you must be fixed and concrete about being - and I call these the D's of the Day. There are a plethora of books on success and I've read a many of them. And no matter how they reword it or sloganize it, these D's are the dominant forces in the lives of those who have and are walking in their purpose and achieving success. If there were a

Bible called success, these three would have their own books.

1. Decision

Decide that no matter how it looks, today is a good day! No matter what the opposition is, it's good and will work out for your good. I don't think many people understand how important a decision about a thing is. Your decision about a thing will determine your mindset. And your mindset creates your action. This then leads to:

2. Direction

Your day has **D**irection because you have spoken over it with prayer and affirmations of what the day must be like. Days are like blank sheets of paper, and until you say something, there is nothing there but room for the enemy or someone else to make it what they want. It's your day to determine what it will be.

3. Discipline

Anybody can make something look good on the surface, and there are many people who have the look of success. The true measure of success is not things. The true measure of success comes from being disciplined. **D**iscipline is doing what needs to be done even when you don't feel like doing it. This is one of the major reasons why people don't reach the plateau of success and for those who do and fail; it can usually be attributed to the loss of the very thing that got them there. Your purpose demands that you be a good steward. This means that you have to become disciplined with being on time, tasks oriented and so on. And there will be times when you don't want to. But discipline will demand that you do it, even when you don't feel like it. The difference between those that become and achieve greatness and those that remain average is not that those great have something extra, or were born with inaccessible talent. The difference maker is **D**iscipline.

4. **Drive**

If you want it, you've got to go and get it! Nobody is just handing out success. **D**rive is having an unfailing, unyielding, vigorous determination to push past any and all obstacles. Dreamers run when others walk because the dreamer has **D**rive. In any relationship there will be challenges - there will be surmounting obstacles - there will even be the plight of wanting to quit and settle for less. But you must acquire the drive to push past any feeling of abandoning your purpose. If you had 500 yards to swim and you swam 250, if you turn around and swim back you just swam the 500. So keep moving forward. It's through drive that you procure that unyielding determination to push past mediocrity to the other side.

Drive is like a second wind. **D**rive is the hydration when you've done your best and the results seem bleak. It's the wind in your sail when nothing seems to be gaining traction. It's the push of courage to take the next step when the one you just took came up short. **D**rive, is the cheer that drowns out the voice of failure. When you lack **D**rive you settle for the status quo and nullify your creative abilities. It is important that you learn how to muster and harness **D**rive because you will not have all the help and supporting cast you start out with. But when you have **D**rive, you have enough and help will show up as you push forward.

5. Dedication

This **D** tops them all. You can have made the **D**ecision, know the **D**irection, acquired the **D**rive and **D**iscipline but if you don't have **D**edication, you will soon burn out in the other four. **D**edication is having the wherewithal to stay committed to a thing until the desired outcome is achieved. **D**edication tells **D**iscipline "It's worth it", to **D**rive it says "We are going to get there", **D**ecision "thanks for the choice" and **D**irection 'we made it". Many people start out with good intentions but are usually running on mere excitement and enthusiasm. Only when you settle in and the realities of the work that must be done to achieve what you saw occurs that you discover that **D**edication is a very needed and important component. As excited as you will be and convinced that you are doing what you were created to do, there will be times of not wanting to do anything at all. There will be times when no matter how much effort you exert, it seems like you aren't moving. But it is in those times that you need the **D**iscipline and the **D**edication of remaining faithful to what you originally set out to do.

If you acquire these D's at the start of your day and allow nothing to shake you off the foundation of your set mandate, you've purposefully positioned yourself to accomplish everything you desire.

respect the small beginning

There is often a feeling of needing bigger to feel better or seeing more to feel accomplished. Nothing has to stay the size that it starts, but everything has to go through its proper stages to get to the place of it being able to support the next size. Dreams and purposes are seen built but that building comes through a process. The key to bigger is being a good steward over the little that's already in hand. It's a universal law that what you do in the least you will also do in the much. So if there is no regard for what little you have then there will be a disregard when there is more.

More only does one thing - it amplifies who you already are. So, if you are accustomed to disregarding process and wanting to scurry through to get to higher ground, you will be the exact same with more. Why do you think parents put more time in with an infant and toddler? Because at that stage of his life, he needs more care and nurturing. It's critical to the developmental process of the child, and at the same time, it is building within the child the trainings they will soon need when they grow up.

> **Right now, you have everything you need. It is possible that you haven't capitalized on it all.**

And so it is with small beginnings. There is no need to rush the process. There are lessons you need to learn and hiccups that you can only afford to make at the small or early stage.

People don't respect the small beginning because they don't understand the difference between potential and capacity. Potential deals with one's ability to do a thing, while one's capacity deals with how much of a thing a person can do with their potential at a given time. The confusion comes when an individual sees more than they can handle. With your potential alone, it may be possible for you to ensure you can handle much more, but capacity advances through the development of the growth from small to great. If you want more, increase your capacity, not your potential.

the greatest of a tree reveals its nurturing as a seed.

Right now I'm doing more than I've ever done before. I had that potential in me all the time. I saw it years before I ever walked in it. But I would never have gotten to the place of having and handling more and more importantly, keeping it, had I not had a respect for those small beginnings. It was there in my home office that I developed the capacity to handle a 13 office complex. If the little is causing chaos and confusion, then you are definitely not ready for a lot. Small beginnings help to develop you. They train you on how to maximize every accessible avenue until you actually have no other way. This then forces the little to expand. In essence, not only are you expanding in purpose, you are expanding your ability to handle more.

While respecting the small beginning, work towards reaching outside the boundaries or color lines. There should always be a fire burning inside of you for more but make sure it's a controlled fire and not a wild fire. Don't disrespect the small beginnings but also don't become trapped by them either. You should be constantly reaching for the next level. You can still reach for the next level while respecting and stewarding where you currently are. Oftentimes for a sense of security it's taught to draw inside the lines but I believe in creating new boundaries. When you've taken every available asset and used it to its fullest capacity, you are reaching outside the color lines. You are putting a demand on the next level. Small beginnings are just that - small beginnings. They are not intended for you to stay that way; they're just a start.

Step

There is tentativeness in the small beginning that if you are not careful, you can get stuck in. This often comes from looking for all the greenlights before you go. What I mean by greenlights is that many times we look for having all that we think the next level needs before we even move in that direction. Truthfully, you come into more as you are moving than you ever will waiting. Even in the small beginning, you need to step. See, no step is too small and even the smallest step is progress. It can take one step to enter a room but ten to fifty to cross it. Had it not been for the one step, you would have not even entered the room. There will be many times when you will need to step, with nothing you need at grasp but believing you'll have all you need by the time your foot lands. You have to step! I've come to learn that what most considered a jump was nothing more than a step. And what was thought to only be a step was a huge jump. You have to step!

> sometimes your biggest is the next step.

It was this one word from my "soon-to-be" mentor that gave me the mustering of faith and courage I needed to obey God and take that one step. I, too, at one time was looking for all greenlights. I knew that I was supposed to start a ministry. I rode around for days crying, knowing what I was supposed to do but too afraid to take the step. One day I came home exhausted from all the agony. I fell on my couch and picked up the remote, just to watch something to get my mind off of it. Just as I turned on my TV, Dr. I.V. Hilliard was on and in perfect timing he said "There is someone that just tuned in, and you are looking for all the lights to be green, but you heard God and what are you waiting for? You have to step and trust that as you place your foot down God will provide the rock to stabilize you." I started crying and laughing all at the same time. That was it! What I was contending with had been exposed. All I was missing was confidence to step without needing a greenlight approval. It's not the greenlights on the outside that you need to see; it's the one on the inside that you must obey. And I had heard the instruction loud and clear. It wasn't that I didn't know what to do, I had to get over the common norm of how I believed things were done. If you know what you should be doing or what the next move should be, standing there won't make it happen or bring it to pass, you have to muster the strength and belief in self to STEP.

Be BOLD!

There is a certain level of boldness that comes with living on purpose. Hear me well, you have nothing to fear or be intimidated about! Let nothing rob you of your confidence or dampen your expectation of achieving greatness. You have got to be bold! We've adopted a negative understanding of being bold and look down on those who are confident in whom they are. What many call being humble is nothing more than standing weak in confidence. It's a masked false perception of humility and it is ruining many of the chance of achieving their purpose. This is a false belief and the sad irony is that those who get trapped in this mode of thinking and way of being become very prideful, judgmental and self-righteous. They often belittle anyone who rises above them and never see the height of success they desire. They also are unhelpful towards others and fend for the spotlight. There is nothing wrong with thinking great of yourself, as long as you are clear with where the ability to such comes from. It's the "me, myself and I" attitude that perverts authentic boldness and the belief in self. You have to be BOLD about who you are! Be BOLD about what you can do! And be BOLD about doing it! The key to boldness is simple;

1. Own it!
2. Commit to the decision.
3. Be it - Do it, with a winner's attitude.
4. Help someone else that's going in the same direction you are.

i Am

i Am confident in my ability to follow through.

i Am a doer and not just a hearer.

i Am a goal setter and I finish what I start.

i Am purpose driven.

i Am not moved by words of my foes.

i Am respecter of my time, treasure, talent and the time of others. I am never late.

i Am respectful and honor those who sow wisdom and knowledge into my life.

i Am honest and hold true to my character and integrity at all cost..

i Am favored and have good fortune.

i Am a Winner.

circle of influence

Many successful people failed in living out their full potential for no other reason than not having the proper circle of influence. I hold this key very dear to my heart, and I respect and honor the position it holds in life for success. The one thing I've discovered about people who really value their growth and achievement is that they are very reputable people and seek the association of the same type of people. They hold themselves to a very high moral standard. It showed me why some continue to climb, others level off, some never get off and others fall off. It was all because of their circle of influence. As I said in an earlier chapter, eagles fly with eagles. Size isn't the factor, it's the identity. If you are going to be in the climbing group, you must protect, honor and value those in your circle of influence because they are just that - influence. When something is an influence to you, it has a bearing on your decision making and your moral compass.

I used to think that all rich and successful people were snooty and looked down on other people. I'm not saying that there isn't a class of rich and successful people who aren't like that; however it wasn't until I joined this group of guys who are very well off, successful business owners that I realized the unity and level of responsibility that they held towards each other. I learned that there is usually abhorrence to something you do not understand. I didn't understand it then, but now I do. This group alone caused me to evaluate the way I do things. I was able to embrace a new mannerism in meeting settings. I attained a level of business lingo that I didn't have before. All of this came from this small group.

On the other hand, you could allow people in your space who contaminate your dreams and aspirations. Once you leave them, you feel drained and depleted rather than encouraged and refueled. I never let people in my space who rob me of my passion for what I do. I'm a problem solver, that's part of my assignment, but there comes a point when I have to realize that they are beyond my influence of assisting and any other attempt to help will only bring a burden on me. You can't have an above average mentality while the conviction of your circle of influence is "just

> intentionally go where you want to grow.

enough". When you leave the company of your most valued friends, you shouldn't feel like you have taken steps backwards. Real friends aren't only for good times but should also pull out the best of you.

Here's how you evaluate your true circle of influence:

1. Do you feel drained or do you feel charged once you're out of their presence?
2. Do you receive anything worth keeping? (wisdom, knowledge, good feeling)
3. Do you feel like you are the one who's always giving?
4. Do you mask who you really are to fit in?
5. Do you discern a change in them from being around you?
6. Does the relationship feel forced?
7. Do you trust them with your private life?
8. Do you hold back sharing your dreams?

If you answered yes to any of these questions, my suggestion is that you reevaluate whether you haven't given an acquaintance the title of a friend.

When it comes to success, you need people of like-mindedness. They don't have to be your friends, but the company you keep is equivalent to the success you attain. For instance, there are leaders who I know, but there are also leaders who I hang around. I understand the dissimilarity in the two relationships and what I look to give and/or get from each. Because I do know the dissimilarity of the two, I am able to be me in both groups while bringing or taking away something from them both. It is for you to know where a person sits relationally in your life. It is for you to set and respect those needed boundaries. Do not hear this as becoming a self-absorbed, hard to get along with, needing to watch everybody person. That is not what I want you to draw from this chapter. But there are people you need in your life and as you walk in your purpose and have success, there will be people who will need you in their life. What I do know is that it is hard to hang around anybody for any length of time and not leave without being influenced by them in some way.

Mentor

There is a proverb that says that *counsel in the heart of man is like water in a deep well, but a man of understanding draws it out*. What this speaks to is the need of you having someone in your life who has been there. No one goes up in an airplane without a skilled pilot. No building is constructed without having first passed through the mind and hands of a skilled architect. As beautiful as the piano is, its purpose is not carried out to completion without the skilled hands of a pianist. Likewise, with as much potential as you have, you need a mentor in your life to help you reach your destiny and fulfill your purpose. People look for and honor the skill in all other areas of life, except in the thing that means the most and that is their purpose. There is someone who has in them what you need.

A mentor is to you, what a coach is to an athlete. The athlete may have the build, the skill and the talent, but it's from the coach where he or she learns how to bring all those qualities together so that the greatness in them can come forth. I wholeheartedly attribute my success and the capacity at which I am able to operate in my purpose to my mentors. I'm often reminded of a statement that my mentor made while I was sitting at his feet to learn. This statement completely revolutionized my life. He said *"that we are the sum total of what others invest in our lives, that we choose to incorporate into our lives."* At that very moment something clicked. Although it was a week-long conference, once I heard that, I could have gone back home. See for years I had been listening but not applying. It was as if I had a mentor but didn't because I wasn't making use out of the wisdom and knowledge that was being given. I got back home and within 6 months, we were doing everything I had written down that I wanted to see happening in the ministry, even down to hiring two staff people, came to fruition. See a wise man will hear and increase in learning and a man of understanding shall attain unto wise counsels.

Who's pouring into you? What more experienced person are you in pursuit of? Why are you trying to learn it all by yourself? There is someone who has gone before you for you and you need to make the connection. Like the proverb said, it's in there but a man of understanding will draw it out. The drawing is from the mentor; you getting to them is your responsibility.

This is a principle far removed from many of this generation because of the loss of honor. So what most try to do is copy and that's why they never walk in the fullness of what they have the potential to become. It's false honor. I'm seeing more young basketball players turn to the old greats for their wisdom and insight on the game. Why? Because "the greats" have been where they desire to go. The wealth of knowledge that they have far exceeds any amount of practices on their own. And the proof is evident. Most of all those who have sought counsel spend more time in the league and lead their teams to triumphant victories.

This is what a mentor provides: A knowledge and skill set that equips you for where you are going. No need in trying to recreate the wheel or blaze a new trail. Find your mentor. The degree of honor and submission you give to someone else, will be the degree and honor that others will give to you.

a time to reflect

You will always need time to reflect. As you grow, the procedures and ways that you currently do things may need changing or adjusting. Those times of reflection allow you to evaluate yourself and what you are currently involved in, and to determine if you are operating at optimum performance. Are there things that could be done better or smarter? Are there things that you don't need to do anymore? Or are there things that you need to do to prepare for what lies ahead? Reflection is that thing that keeps you ahead of the curve, engaged in the times, equipped and on the cusp of vision success. You need a time to reflect.

A word that parallels to reflect is study. So when you reflect, you are studying and we know what the outcome of studying does. It makes you more knowledgeable and coherent in an area. So through reflecting, you become better at what you do, hence making what you do better.

Major Fortune 500 companies do it all the time - that's why they are the leading companies. They reflect constantly to keep themselves abreast of change and demand. When I go sit at the feet of my pastor and mentors, I am reflecting. When I do surveys to get feedback from the people I minister and speak to, I am reflecting. See, a time to reflect isn't just an isolated event or moment; you can reflect as you go. When we first started, I felt that it was imperative that the vision be deep-seated in the people. So we set out with a plan of getting it committed to memory. It started out well, but as we increased, we took on people at different learning curves. Based on my reflection I realized that I had to deviate from my initial plan which led to the development of a shorter, catchy, more precise vision. Presented it to my team and they loved it. Next thing we did was position a big day around it with a new logo to match and boy it was great! Now if you ask anyone what our vision is, they no longer have to use the old paragraph to explain it. In one short and catchy phrase they would say "We are Discipling Believers to REACH Out, LIVE Out, and BE Out for the Kingdom of God." That came through my taking time to reflect.

You can't be afraid to change an idea or a way of doing a thing if the way it is being done no longer produces the same results. We can actually avoid many of the setbacks we face if we would do more reflecting. You have to gauge the nature of the business or career that you are in and this will set the degree at how often you need time to reflect.

Lastly, you need a time to reflect for you. There is a divine or established order, and we should work just as hard to keep it in place. And when you are operating in your purpose it is easy to rearrange that order. The proper order is God, spouse, kids, job, family then friends. If any of these are out of order, you are out of order. It's not true success if don't know your kids and you lose your spouse along the way. You are selfish and you are only good at what you want. We never have to sacrifice God, or family for success. So a part of reflecting is to do self-examination to see if you are keeping your life in order. There will be times of sacrifice that comes with any walk of life but if something is lost, that's not sacrifice, that's negligence, which proves that you are lacking in stewardship.

> if you reflect now, you can avoid having to say later "I should have"

I absolutely love what I do! I am into people. I love encouraging and ministering into the lives of people. My career is time and people consumed. But it is my responsibility to ensure that it does not take precedent over the things that come before what I am purposed to do. When I keep the divine order in place, I am actually better at what I do. And you can't do it all. You need time to rest and reflect. I'll talk more about rest with Key Ten.

Meditate

You need time to meditate. Our minds function better when we step away to a quiet place and take time to reflect. This awakens your creative edge and allows you to get a 3D look at you and what you are involved in.

Usually when we are hands on, we don't see everything. I have an excellent strategy team and they get the job done. But it's always someone that comes back to the table with a better way or better idea and it's because I encourage that we meditate on the task at hand. When we take time and get quiet, we position ourselves to see and hear more. Think over your plan of action. You may see something that you didn't see at first.

You need meditation because when you think right you do right. I have a hundred ideas going through my mind daily. But when I meditate I am able to differentiate and filter out those things that are just mere thoughts versus those things that are being downloaded into my spirit for taking action on. Meditation is that clarifying time that we each need. It's that time of filing and purging your mental file cabinets.

Get a Journal

You must write out your thoughts. The more you get off the mind, the more room you afford for the receiving of more ideas. It is not good work or a good business habit to carry vision around only in your mind. You need a written point of reference for the things you receive concerning your life, career, family and future. The mind is powerful. But the mind has better functionality and you get the most out of your mind when you allow it the impulsiveness to focus on one thing at a time. And this is what journaling allows you to do. It frees the mind of having to remember that while focusing on this. Some of the greatest ideas are often lost because instead of writing it out, the person tried to commit it to memory while remembering the last thing they thought of and completing the thing they're in. If you write it down, you are now assured you won't forget; you can come back to them when you're ready and you can fully focus on the task at hand.

Lastly, as you are living on purpose, there will be times when it seems like nothing is working. You may even question whether or not you are doing the right thing. The beauty of journaling is that you can always go back and get the encouragement to press on because you can clearly see the words from the Almighty that told you what to do.

Confess

Our word shapes our world and words do the very same thing to you. Your tongue can be your advocate or your adversary. You have to be cautious of the words you speak. That's why I included the "Motivational Confessions" in this book. Meditation is speaking in the mind. Confession is speaking from the mind. If I listen to you talk long enough, I can tell you how much you believe in you and inevitably how your life is going to turn out. When you speak, your words are laying out a course that your foot work will follow. No doubter speaks success and no successful person speaks doubt.

Because we face hard times and perplexities, it doesn't mean we have to speak of or on them. I believe that death (the fall of the person) and life (the success of the person) is in their tongue. Think of the number of men and women who have or still battle with low self-esteem for no other reason than what was or wasn't said to them or from negativity continuously spoken over their lives. Your words matter. If you don't want to see it, then why continue to speak it. You are either going to be justified by your words or condemned by them. Quickly identify the difference between words of concern and words of doubt. Don't allow your time to be consumed with talking about what you don't have or how terrible things are looking. Those are the facts, and facts are subject to change. Confess what you want to see not what you see. People of purpose speak with purpose.

i Will

i Will not allow mediocrity to pass through my hands. Everything gets my best.

i Will not allow my life to be governed by the dictates of others.

i Will never settle for commonplace.

i Will give back by helping others.

i Will always remain ready to seize every favorable opportunity.

i Will handle and treat every situation like it matters most.

i Will keep my word at all cost.

i Will not bring disgrace, maltreatment or degradation on others to achieve growth.

i Will never bring shame, disrespect or dishonor to anything or anyone left to my care.

i Will always acknowledge God as the source of my supply.

Key Eight

focus

It is important that as a person of purpose that you remain focused. You cannot afford to get lost in the cloud of clutter or caught up in sideline distractions. The cloud of clutter is when you have so many irons in the fire until you can't give the most earnest attention to

> every tree
> you see was
> once a seed
> under the
> ground.

what needs it now. You have to know your limit. I've encountered many people who find it rather flattering to announce how many things they are working on at one time, to give the impression of success. But the only people they are impressing are themselves. The proof is always in the results. They are in the cloud of clutter and the hope is that at least one of them will gain momentum. But how can any of it come to full fruition if you are not giving it the undivided attention and personal touch it needs? There is also the false presumption that by working on everything at the same time, everything will take off at the same time and the many streams can all flow together. But let me tell you that it never works out that way. This mindset comes as a result of the sideline distraction and proves why focus is very important.

Sideline distractions occur when a person compares him/herself to the progression of someone else and even tries to keep up or thrive on their level. If you cannot appreciate the success of someone else without trying to be them, it is a clear indication that you are not ready for success. There will be many people who are ahead of you in some way or another. We have successors in every field of life. If you allow your focus to be drawn away from what you should be doing inorder to try to operate on a level that others have proven over time that they are prepared to be on, you are going to sink your ship before it even leaves the port. It is at that moment that you have succumbed to a spirit of competition, which is a sideline distraction. Competition is not a key of functioning in purpose or achieving success. You have to be the best you and continue to grow and expand in what and who you've been chosen to be. When you lose focus and begin to compete, you are not growing in your own authentic self, but you are looking at what others are doing which now has you in a "keeping up" mentality. Competing causes:

   a. A loss of vision.
   b. The incorporation of unneeded tasks and agendas.
   c. Money being wasted.
   d. An illusion of success.
   e. The perpetration of premature platforms.
   f. Dead ends.

Focus is a major key to staying in purpose. You have to have just as much excitement about the unlimited possibilities and potential that lies within you as you have with looking at what others have already accomplished. Keep in mind that they were at the same point as you are, and they had to acquire the same disciplines to get to where they are. Any tree that you can now see had to have once been a seed under the soil. Don't become distracted by the success of others. It would actually do you good to celebrate them. There is nothing wrong with seeing what others are doing and even pull some ideas that can improve on what you are doing, but don't allow your focus to be pulled away from what matters most and that's your unique purpose. Stay focused!

This is where Key One will be such a help to you. When you have defined your river (purpose), it acts as a guard rail so as to keep you in line and on track with what you should be doing. There is always a tendency to want to jump on the bandwagon of the hottest thing. But the problem is you don't know when or where it stops. And most of the time, it's the next stop. Always remember success is a process, so don't allow the get rich schemes to deter and cloud your focus.

Master Your Lane

It's a sad reality that many people who want success tend to be more focused on the accomplishments of others, rather than on their own. We are in a culture where people love to live through the dreams and success of others. But this is not the proper order of life and never yields the success desired. It is cancerous to your purpose. You have a lane to master and focusing on what others are doing in their lane will cause your lane to become unrecognizable to you. When you spend time focusing on what other people are doing and how successful they have become in their lane, your lane becomes unfamiliar to you, undesirable and even harder to get back in. Such actions can easily result in your having an aversion to your true self. You have a lane in life that you have been called to, and it has within it as much influence and attention as you are giving to others in their lane. There may be a plethora of things that you can do but there is that something that you are great at and this is the lane that you need to be in. Even on highways, it's a violation to drive in the other person's lane. And when it comes to purpose the rule yet applies. Do not become the "Jack of all trades, master of none." There is something you were born to master!

When you fail to master your lane, you are treating it as if it is irrelevant. Your lane matters! It is just as important as the other lanes that you see. Perhaps they look better because the other drivers focused on making their lanes better, bigger and longer. You can do the same for your lane. But first, you must be willing to give it the attention it initially needs. Begin by taking your eyes off of the lanes of others. Don't get fixated on what they are doing in their lanes. It's okay to gain encouragement and even ideas from others, but there is a lane that is yours and it is yours to master. You were born to master your lane. Are you ready!

Key Nine

bake your own cake

There are thousands of recipes for cakes and not one person thinks any less of their recipe than someone else. Some people have so much faith in their recipe that it's considered to be a family secret and is passed down from generation to generation. And just think; it's only a cake recipe. I initially wanted to call this chapter "Dare to be Different" because that is what it's referring to, but after much thought, I decided that if I was going to talk about daring to be different, then why not have a chapter title that's different.

I've come across so many people who trash their dreams because of the vast number of people who are doing the same thing. SO WHAT! This may be true, but nobody does it like you. Your purpose will always have a place and be the solution for someone. When you go to the store, think of the different cakes you have to choose from? Now how many more choices could you have if the others thought just as much about their recipe as those who were bold enough to share theirs with the world? And how many of the ones that are being sold could have missed out on the opportunity had they counted themselves out by looking at those that were already being sold? Are you getting my cakes conversation? It's not as much about the cake as it is about the person who believes in it.

There are unique qualities about each of us and it's these qualities that set us apart. Being relevant doesn't exclude being different. It's like each recipe having its own special ingredient. And it's that, that sets your cake apart from others.

In success, you have to be daring enough to bake your own cake. There will always be the crowd who will play it safe and go with the status quo. But I believe that you see yourself as being more than just average.

I was having a session with a new mentee who is attending college under the advice of someone else and to please her parents. Immediately as we started our session she started crying. Well, I'm accustomed to that - I knew what it was because I've seen that cry a many of times. She was eating cake. See, there is no joy or happiness when you are living how others want you to live and not how you know you are supposed to. It's frustrating and bears no sentiment of development. That's eating cake. You're just taking what's being served. Once we got through the tears and I began to ask some challenging questions to help hone in on what she liked most, we discovered that she was a hairstylist. Can you believe that she was

> we all have that one single ingredient that sets us apart, even if it all looks the same.

even told that it didn't matter what she got a degree in? Just get a degree - Wow!

Once we discovered what cake to bake, we ran into another problem; she was considering all the other cakes that were already on display and figured that there wasn't any room for her. I shared with her some of what I'm sharing with you. I had to get her to consider that if all the customers were taken and there were no more cakes, then why were there still schools with students in them? And why would she be willing to take a chance on the advice of others rather than going with what she was creatively and uniquely qualified to do? She was talking to the right person because I had a very successful career in the hair business. So I started talking about the business and the great success and awards I achieved. How I baked my own cake and opened my own shop with no money and gained huge notoriety. I explained to her that it is never about the current cakes you see. There is always room for one more. The tears became a smile and we begin to devise a plan to get her in her river. She stopped eating and started baking. The timing was perfect. The very next month she was able to enroll in beauty school and became one of the top students in her class - just like that. She is as excited as ever and even has clients that come to the school that ask just for her. Out of all the cakes, they want the one she bakes. See what you miss when you eat what's served rather than baking your own cake. She now has within her own control the power to chart her own course of life and not accept what's served.

Your purpose can seem like a daring feat, but you have the ability to do it. It's your unique difference (that special ingredient) that makes you unlike any other. The key is buying in to you. You have to be your first customer. Question - if you are eating cake, where did it come from? I'll tell you - from a person daring enough to bake.

enjoy living

I have been waiting to get you here. I am an avid reader and no book I've ever read on purpose talks about this. I am convinced that enjoying life is vitally important to your success. You are at your best when you are at rest. None of it matters if you can't enjoy living while enjoying purpose. People spend all of their lives building their careers and lose sight of what it means to enjoy life. They don't know how to pull away from the computer or leave the work environment. Don't become that person - work should not consume you. The key is that at every stage of development, enjoy where you are. That's what makes work worth living.

> living life also includes enjoying the journey.

I used to be so consumed that even on vacation I would take work. The one time I didn't take any work, I felt like I was cheating myself, not realizing that by bringing work I actually was cheating myself. Trust me; you get more done enjoying life, than you do letting life run you. Rest is so important that we have a day called rest.

Living on Purpose is a journey with many working components, and you don't have to fear or negate enjoying living while you are evolving into the person you purposed to be. Your mind and body needs time to vacate - to totally shut off, shut down and shut away from anything that sounds like work. Rest allows your brain to have the needed downtime to replenish its store of attention. You'll come back motivated with a fresh vigor, a new outlook, a better sense of creativity and even an excitement for purpose. I always feel new when I get back from vacation or time off. As I re-approach job assignments and tasks, I always feel like I am putting fresh eyes and hands on them. Having always given all of me, I felt like I was giving all of a new and rested me in the sense of having given my body and mind the time to recalibrate.

I can't say it enough - ENJOY LIVING! Yes - work hard but play hard also. And just like you mandate your day and set goals, you need to plan for times of enjoyment. If nothing else, take a day to banish yourself from all work related tasks. I promise you, this may not sound befitting to success but studies have proven that the brain requires substantial downtime to remain industrious and generate its most innovative ideas. And that people who work excessive hours see the return in bad health and emotional distress. I say again - ENJOY LIVING! Just like you put energy and time into planning your success, be that same person in putting time and energy into your time of rest.

Conclusion

For we are God's [own] handiwork (His
workmanship), recreated in Christ Jesus, [born anew]
that we may do those good works which God
predestined (planned beforehand) for us [taking
paths which He prepared ahead of time], that we
should walk in them [living the good life which He
prearranged and made ready for us to live].

Ephesians 2:10AMP

Throughout this entire book, I have been sharing with you keys of success and purpose from the Word of God. I believe God had me to write it this way to show you how easy it is to incorporate the Word of God in your daily life and how God is equally concerned about your purpose and destiny in life. It's ironic that people only see the Word of God as a rule book and never realize that the Word of God has so much more to offer and to say about your daily life and purpose. It is so rich with wisdom and information, but if you have been conditioned to only see it as a religious book, then you miss the full essence of what the Bible affords.

Although most of all the secular books you read get the foundation of what they write from the Word, what many go to schools and pay thousands of dollars for is usually sitting right on their coffee table or book shelf but never apprehended. It's the greatest success book you will ever read. All manner of wisdom gets it foundation from the Word of God. So we don't have to look away from the Word for what we need to be successful; we can look to the Word. It is filled with many success business stories. From a merchant marine like Peter, a lumber salesman and world renowned guidance counselor like Solomon, to even CEOs like Joseph and Daniel, the Word is full of examples of the successes of people who walked in the fullness of their purpose.

Never feel immoral or condemned about wanting more or wanting success. You inherited that from your Heavenly Father. Success is God's will for you. Where do you think you got the desire from? His thoughts towards you are for success and His desire for you is to increase. Make it your everyday goal to live on purpose. YOU WEREN'T CREATED TO FAIL; ONLY TO SUCCEED!

Start Here - like NOW

Psalms 102:13 - *now is the time*
Proverbs 6:6-11 - *purpose happens on purpose*
Ecclesiastes 3:1 – *you have a purpose*
Jeremiah 1:5 - *you are in purpose*
Acts 4:13 - *education doesn't define purpose*
II Corinthians 6:2 - *you are now in purpose*
Proverbs 16:9 - *exercise of purpose*

Key One - defining the river

Genesis 2:10-14 - *the river led to resources*
Genesis 12:1-3, Judges 13:5, I Samuel 16:1-13,Luke 1:31-33, 4:18, 5:10, Galatians 1:15-16 - *something you are ordained to master*
Joshua 1:8 - *good success*
Proverbs 18:16 - *your gift makes room*
Jeremiah 29:11 - *seek God for purpose (river) not man*
John 15:8, 10 - *purposed to bring forth fruit*
Ephesians 2:10 - *recreated for good works*
Genesis 30:26-43 - *Entrepreneur - Jacob*

Key Two - the belief in self

Philippians 1:13AMP
Ephesians 3:20, I John 4:4 - *it starts within*
Psalms 27:13, II Corinthians 4:18, I John 3:3 - *believe it before you see it*
Mark 9:23, 10:27 - *fear success*

I Samuel 17:31-37, Mark 10:27, Luke 17:6, Philippians 1:6, 2:13, 4:13, Colossians 1:10-11, Hebrews 12:1-3 - *believing that you can*
Psalms 18:29, Isaiah 40:31, 54:4, Mark 11:23 - *don't allow the mountain to defeat you*

Know Your Worth

Numbers 13:25-33, Luke 17:21, John 1:12, Romans 8:16, 37, Ephesians 1:4, I Peter 1:9, I John 3:2, 4:17, 5:4

Raising the Success Ceiling

Genesis 13:14-15, Proverbs 23:7, Isaiah 54:2-3, Matthew 25:14-23,29, Luke12:48 16:10

Self-Investment

Joshua 1:8, Proverbs 1:5, 3:1318, 4:5-9, 18:9,19:24,24:30-34, 26:13-15, Ecclesiastes 10:18, Romans 12:11, Ephesians 4:28, Hebrews 6:12

Keep Learning

Proverbs 9:9, 16:23, Acts 17:11, Titus 3:14, I Thessalonians 4:11, I Timothy 4:15, II Timothy 2:15

Stay Ahead

Proverbs 6:6-8, 24:27, Matthew 1-13, Luke 12:42-44, John 16:13

Give Your Best

Proverbs 13:4, 14:23, 18:19, 21:25, Ecclesiastes 9:10, 10:18, Matthew 5:16, 41, 9:37, 25:15,20, Luke 16:10-11, Ephesians 6:5-8, Colossians 3:23-24

Be On Time

Psalms 90:12, Proverbs 6:6-11, 25:19, 26:14, Ecclesiastes 3:1, Mark 13:33-37, Matthew 24:1-13, I Corinthians 16:3, Titus 3:1

Keeping Your Word

Psalms 138: 2, Proverbs 20:25, 25:14, 19, Ecclesiastes 5:2-7, Numbers 23:19,30:2-4, Isaiah 55:10-11, Matthew 5:33-37

Look Your Best

Genesis 1:26, I Samuel 16:7, II Kings 10:1-10, Luke 15:21-22, II Timothy 2:15

Past Failures

Philippians 1:13-14, Isaiah 41:13, 43:18, Psalms 23, 121

Size Bullying

Genesis 13:14-15, 18:14, I Samuel 14:6, Chap.17 - Joshua 6:1-2

"What If" Question

Philippians 4:6-8, Matthew 11:28-30, I Peter 5:7, Hebrews 4:16AMP

Meeting the Status Quo

II Corinthians 10:12-14, Romans 12:3, 6

Key Three - goal the vision

Habakkuk 2:2-3 - *vision must be written down*
Luke 14:28 - *vision and planning comes first*
Psalms Chap. 23, 32:8
Proverbs 19:20 - *setting goal manifest the latter end*
Proverbs 4:13 - *Life comes out of instructions*
Proverbs 29:18 - *restraint without vision*

Setting Goals
II Chronicles 15:7, Psalm 20:4, 33:11, 127:1, Proverbs 16:3,9, 19:21, 21:5, 24:27, Isaiah 32:8

Key Four - mandate the day

Deuteronomy 4:39, 8:18 - *define the purpose the day*
Psalms 90:12,118:24 - *capitalize on today's opportunity*
Proverbs 13:2-3 - *slothfulness leads to nothing*
Matthew 6:33:34 - *take it one day at a time/each day prepares for the next*

Decision
Deuteronomy 30:19
Joshua 24:15
I Samuel 15:22
Matthew 6:24

Direction
I Kings 17:1-9
Psalms 119:23, 133
Proverbs 3:6, 11:5

Discipline
Proverbs 4:20-27, 20:4, 13
Luke 9:62
I Corinthians 15:58
II Corinthians 9:8
Galatians 5:1, 7
Titus 2:7
Hebrews 12:2

Drive
Isaiah 54:17
Mark 2:3-5, 5:25-29
Acts 5:20-42, 14:19-20
Romans 8:35-39

Dedication
I Samuel 31:4-5
II Kings 2:1-13
Ecclesiastes 7:8-10
Colossians 3:17

Key Five - respect the small beginning

Job 8:7 - *things start small*
Proverbs 12:,14,24 - *work with your hands*
Zechariah 4:10 - *don't look down on small beginnings*
Matthew 25:21-23 - *faithfulness over little rewards rulership over much*
Mark 4:26-29 - *from seed to tree*
Luke 16:10, 19:13-26 - *good stewardship increases occupancy*

Step
Proverbs 12:27, Jeremiah 1:6-10, Matthew 14:26-29, Ephesians 3:12, 6:10, Philippians 1:6, Hebrews 3:14, 10:35, I Peter 5:10

Be BOLD!
I Samuel 17:32-51, Psalms 56:11, 118:6, Matthew 16:18-19, John 1:16AMP, Romans 8:31, 35-39, Ephesians 6:10, Philippians 4:13, II Timothy 1:7, Hebrews 4:16, 10:19-23,35, I John 4:4,

Key Six - circle of influence

Exodus 18:14-19, 23-24 - *success and peace through wise counsel*
I Kings 12:6-16 - *unwise counsel leads to lost*
Psalms 26:4-5, I Corinthians 15:33 - *good manners can be corrupted*
Proverbs 1:5, 10-18 - *a man of understanding attains to wise counsel*

Proverbs 2:1-5, 4:20-27 - *counsel rewards*
Proverbs 11:14, 13:20 15:22 - safety *and establishment/become wise*
Proverbs 13:7, 20 - *walk with the wise*
Proverbs 14:7 - *stay around knowledge*
II Corinthians 13:5 - *befitting to self-examine*

Mentor

[Exodus 24:13, Numbers 11:28, Deuteronomy 21:7-8,34:9], I Kings 19:19-21, Proverbs 9:9, 13:18, 25, 17:27, 20:5, 22:6, 27:17, Jeremiah 3:15, Luke 24:45, I Corinthians 4:15, Titus 2:6-8

Key Seven - a time to reflect

Proverbs 11:1 - *keep balance*
Proverbs 25:2 - *examination of matters*
Mark 6:30, Luke 10:17 - *know what's working and assess accomplishments or shortcomings.*
Proverbs 14:8 - *understanding your way*
Luke 16:2 - *account for the organization of our undertakings*
Luke 19:15 - *oversight and assessment*
John 6:10-12 - *organization, structure and accountability*
I Timothy 4:13-15 - *cultivating is important*

Meditate

Genesis 24:63, Joshua 1:8, Psalms 1:2, 49:3, 63:6, 104:34, 119:15, 143:5, Proverbs 4:26, Haggai 1:5, I Timothy 4:15

Get a journal

Exodus 17:14, 32:32, Isaiah 8:1, 30:8, Habakkuk 2:2, Luke 4:17, I Timothy 4:13-16, II Timothy 3:16

Confess
Numbers 23:19, Proverbs 13:2-3, 18:20-21, Joshua 1:8, 22:28, Matthew 12:35-37, Mark 11:22-23, James 3:10

Key Eight - focus

Genesis 3:6, Genesis 19:17, 26 - *being deterred*
Joshua 6:1-2, Hebrews 11:1, 6-10, 27 - *see what's yet seen*
Proverbs 4:26-27 - *attentiveness and avoids derailment*
I Samuel 16:6-7 - *proper choice*
Galatians 5:7 - *prevent hindrances.*

Master Your Lane
Daniel 1:3-4, 8-15, 17, I Samuel 17:38-40, 49-50, II Corinthians 13:5

Key Nine - bake your own cake

Genesis 4:2 - *unique quality*
Romans 12:3-5 - *special measure*
Genesis 10:9, Luke 1:17, 32-33, 4:18, Romans 11:13 - *purposed for something specific*

Proverbs 18:16 - *gifted*

Key Ten - enjoy living

Psalms 23 - *the Shepherds care of His sheep*
Mark 6:31 - *vacation is Biblical*
Ecclesiastes 3:22, 5:18-20 - *you should enjoy the fruit of your labour*
John 10:10 - *abundant life overflowing is God's will*
Mark 2:27, Hebrews 4:9-11 - *rest is God's Covenant Promise to the Believer*

Other Books by
Vincent Robinson

Born To Win - *50 Day Business Devotional*

Why Are you Not Filled?

You Can Do it!

Command You Day - *Confessions/Prayer Journal*

God Won't Miss You, But Will You Miss God

Sow - *The Power of a Seed*
The Law of Seedtime and Harvest

i3 eMPOWERMENT mANUAL

For more information, teaching material or partnership, go to
our website at:

rwccc.org

Robinson **M**edia & **P**ublishing

www.ingramcontent.com/pod-product-compliance
Lightning Source LLC
Chambersburg PA
CBHW072043040426
42447CB00012BB/2997